The Best Round Card Games

The Best Round Card Games

TOM KING
"Joker"

LONDON
W. FOULSHAM & CO. LTD.
NEW YORK . TORONTO . CAPE TOWN . SYDNEY

W. FOULSHAM & Co. Ltd.,
2-5 Old Bond Street, London, W.1.

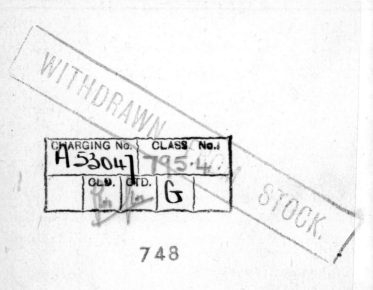

CONTENTS

FOREWORD

Good round card games provide excellent entertainment for parties, social evenings and for family gatherings. There are countless numbers and variations of such games, but in this book we have collected forty-five of the best known card games for a number of players. Even then, people who have played any of these games may find the rules vary slightly, as in many of the popular round games the rules have never been stabilised. However, the versions given in this book are those most generally used, and provided they are explained to each player before play commences, there should be no "comeback".

Whilst some of the games will be found to be suitable for adults only, others—such as Old Maid, Pelmanism, etc.—can be played and enjoyed by all the members of the family.

The pack to be used in all the games described herein is the ordinary 52-card pack, and where jokers or extra cards are needed, full instructions have been given. In certain cases, i.e. Catch-the-Ten, part only of the pack is used; whilst in other instances two or more packs may be needed. At the beginning of each game, however, the number and style of the cards to be used will be clearly indicated. Also at the beginning of each game will be found a note indicating the number of players who may take part in that particular game.

Some of the games are games of skill, others rely purely on chance, and a few are a combination of both. But whichever is the case, it is strongly advised that to gain the most enjoyment from a game of cards, and especially these round games where a number of players take part, the matter should not be taken too seriously. After all, the main idea is to have a little relaxing entertainment and there is no need to treat a card game as a matter of life and death. On the other hand, nothing is more irritating than the card player whose attention is continually wandering from the game or who, throughout the game, keeps up an incessant and endless flow of idle chitter-chatter. Above all things, avoid "post-mortems" at the end of a game. Nothing can be gained by such remarks as "You must have known I held the queen, so I don't understand why you led the king", or by a wholesale dissection of everyone's hand. If mistakes have been made or bad play has occurred, it is unfortunate, but not all the recriminations will put things right; in fact they will only make a bad situation worse. These remarks apply particularly when a game is played for small stakes of money. It is bad luck when a sum of money is lost, perhaps through someone else's stupidity, but it is one of the hazards in any game of chance and it should be treated as such. If you don't want to lose money, then don't join card games which call for stakes or alternatively, have it agreed that the party plays for tokens only.

When a dealer has to be selected, there are several approved methods for doing so, and any of the recognised methods can be used. The most usual is for each player to cut the pack, the person turning up the highest card to be the dealer (the ace can count high or low according to the wishes of the players, but it should be established *before* the cuts are made, which way it is to count). Another method is for each person in turn to draw a card off the top of the pack. The first one to draw a jack is then the dealer.

The Best Round Card Games

1. ADDO

Number of Players: Any number.
Cards: Full pack of 52 cards.

A DEALER is selected by any approved method and the complete pack is dealt out to each player in turn.

The player on the left of the dealer starts first and lays down any card, the value of the card being immaterial. The next player on the left must then aim at laying a card, *of the opposite colour* which, with the previous player's card, gives a total of seven, ten or fifteen, either by addition or subtraction. For this purpose a jack counts as eleven, a queen twelve and a king thirteen; the ace counts one.

Thus if the first player has played a red jack, the second could put down a black four, making fifteen by addition, or a black ace making ten by subtraction.

If he suceeds in "making", the player of the first card must give him a counter. If, however, he cannot "make", he plays any card he chooses and no payment is forthcoming.

It is now the third player's turn. He looks at the second card played and tries to make seven, ten or fifteen with one from his own hand (always playing a card of the opposite colour). Thus the game proceeds, the deal passing in rotation when each player has exhausted his hand.

The game can be made still more interesting by ruling that the following payments be made: one counter for making seven, two counters for making ten, and three for making fifteen.

Two typical Addo combinations:

Jack (11) − Ace (1) = 10
King (13) + Two = 15

2. AUCTION PITCH

Number of Players: Up to seven.
Cards: Full pack plus one joker.

THIS game belongs to the Whist family and has a large following in the United States.

The dealer is selected, as normally, and after cutting and shuffling the cards deals six cards to each player. The cards are dealt out in two lots of three, not singly as is more usual.

The game consists of playing six rounds, each being a trick made up of not four cards, as in ordinary Whist, but of as many cards as there are people sitting round the table.

The player on the dealer's immediate left, looks at his hand and declares which suit shall be trumps. If he chooses, he may sell the privilege of naming trumps to anyone who makes him the best offer. This privilege is worth one, two or perhaps three points, but never more.

The offer to sell, if exercised, goes round the table to the left. All bids must be higher than any previous bid, but a player is not obliged to bid. He may pass.

If the first player sells the privilege of naming trumps, the points given to him are added to his score. But the points he receives may never be sufficient to enable him to finish the game and win. A "game" is ten points and a bid may never take the seller beyond nine points.

If the first player refuses to sell, he must make four points with the hand he is holding.

Whoever buys the right of naming trumps must make as many points with the hand he is holding as he gave for the right of naming trumps.

The first card led in play is put down by the player on the dealer's left or, if he sells the right of naming trumps, by the player who bought the right from him. The first card led is always trumps.

When trumps are led whether in the first or any other round, all other players must follow suit when they can. But when non-trump suits are led, a player may trump, if he likes, although he has a card of the led-suit in his hand.

The highest card of the led-suit wins the round, except when trumped, when the highest trump wins. The winner of each trick leads for the next round.

A hand being finished, the scoring is reckoned as follows:

(a) One point for the player to whom the highest trump is dealt.

(b) One point for the player to whom the lowest trump is dealt.

(c) One point for the player winning the trick which includes the jack of trumps (if it occurs, which is not certain, since all the cards are not dealt).

(d) One point for the player who makes the most in the cards of his winning tricks. For this purpose, the cards are assessed as follows: tens count as ten each; aces count four each; kings count three each; queens count two each; jacks count one each; all other cards count nothing. It must be understood, however, that whatever this total comes to, the holder of the highest amount scores only one point.

(e) One point for the player who takes the joker in a trick.

The player who first makes ten points, wins the game.

3. AUTHORS

Number of Players: Up to ten people.
Cards: Full pack of 52 cards.

THE pack of cards is shuffled, and dealt in the usual way. The whole pack must be used and if a few players have one card each more than the rest, it will not affect the play to any extent.

When the cards have been dealt, the players look at their hands and the one sitting on the left of the dealer has the privilege of commencing. The aim is to obtain sets of cards alike in threes—three jacks, three eights, three twos and so on. The first player may have in his hand at the outset, one or perhaps even more sets of three. If so he lays them face up on the table and they count one point per set in his favour.

But what is practically certain is that his hand consists of some pairs and odd cards. These he must endeavour to change into trebles by exchanging.

The method of exchange is as follows. He turns to any player in the company and says "Please give me a six", or whatever value card he wants.

In asking for this card he must already hold one or two cards of the same value in his hand.

The player to whom the request for a card is made must comply if he holds such a card in his hand, even if it means breaking up a pair or even a three which he is holding.

On handing over the requested card, the player is given another card from the hand of the person making the request.

When the player who asks gets what he wants, he has the privilege of making a second request. The second request may be made of any other player or even from the one who was originally asked.

When a player is asked for a card which he does not

possess, the privilege of making the next request passes to him, and he at once lays down any sets of three which he may already hold in his hand.

The game stops when it is apparent that no more threes can be made. The winner is he who has managed to form the greatest number of threes.

Note that suits do not enter into the calculation, also that there is no rotation of play. Anyone may be called upon without any sort of turn after the game has been opened by the player on the dealer's left.

4. BACCARAT

Number of Players: Any number up to 20.
Cards: Three to six packs.

THIS game is played in two forms: Baccarat Banque, which is described here, and Baccarat Chemin-de-Fer, which is described later in the book.

The players are divided as usual into punters and a dealer. The dealer is decided upon in the first instance by putting the "bank" up for auction, the person who is prepared to risk the largest sum receiving the privilege of being the banker or dealer. He must put the whole sum that he has nominated down on the table in front of him and he may retire from the position of banker when he wishes. He is then succeeded either by the next player in turn, if that player is willing to put up a sum equivalent to the last "bank", or the deal may be auctioned again.

The players sit on both sides of the dealer. Twenty constitute a full table. They may not bet collectively more than the bank which is before the dealer; the amount of this varies, as the dealer is bound to leave all his winnings in the "bank". The player immediately on the dealer's right bets first. He may bet the full amount of the bank, but usually does not. After he has bet the player on the dealer's immediate left may bet to the "uncovered" balance of the bank. Subsequently the next player on the dealer's right, then the next player on the dealer's left, and so on, make their bets, each being limited by the balance remaining "uncovered" when his turn comes up. If all the players together do not put up an amount equivalent to the bank, the dealer may remove the difference from his bank.

All bets are made before cards are dealt. From three to six packs of cards are used. Each player may shuffle in turn. The dealer deals the first card to the player on his right, the second to the player on his left and the third to himself. Then another to the right, one to the left and one to himself. All cards are dealt face down. When the deal is complete the dealer first inspects his cards, and then the other two players do likewise.

It will be observed that however many players there are only the dealer and his two neighbours right and left, receive cards. Each of these two players represents all those who are seated on the same side. And his play is on *behalf of the side*. Consequently rigid conventions must be observed.

Nine is the highest and the winning score at Baccarat, eight being next best, and so on. The ace counts as one, plain cards according to their face value, and court cards as tens. The tens are, however, ignored in reckoning the score. Thus a king and two are counted as two only. A jack and six are reckoned as six. Nine and eight are seven, and queen and eight as eight. A score of ten or twenty is called "Baccarat" and is entirely ignored. It will be seen, therefore, that it is impossible to get *more* than nine.

If, upon inspection of the two cards dealt, the dealer or either of the players finds he holds a "natural" eight or nine he must turn his cards up and announce the fact at once. If the dealer has a natural he wins all the stakes unless there is another natural in which case he wins if he is the higher or loses if he is the lower. If the naturals are equal the bets on that side are "off".

When the dealer has not a natural he announces that he "gives". The two players may each in turn have one card, or they may "stand". After giving the cards required face upwards, the dealer may also have one if he wishes. He then announces his score (or point as it is called) and the other players show theirs. The nearest to nine as between dealer and punter wins; equal scores cancel out.

As an illustration; suppose the dealer is A and the right and left players B and C respectively. B receives in the deal a king and three, C receives four and two, and A a ten and five. The dealer would "give". B would draw one card, say an eight, making his score $10 + 3 + 8 = 21$, the twenty being ignored, his score counts one. C should stand with the score of $4 + 2 = 6$. The dealer A may draw if he wishes; he would probably do so and get, say, a three, making his score $10 + 5 + 3 = 18$, ignoring the ten giving eight points. The other players showing their points as 1 and 6 respectively, the dealer would receive all stakes.

The rigid convention mentioned above applies to the drawing of the extra card by the punter. If his point be six or seven, he will refuse the draw. If it be less than five, he will accept. If it is actually five he may accept or decline. Any other course of play, since his action influences the fate of other people's stakes, is against the recognised procedure. In some circles a breach of these principles is punished by a fine, or even compelling the offender to pay the stakes of the other players if they should be lost.

The hand being complete, the used cards are thrown into a waste basket. The deal is made, as before, from the unused cards, except that if either or both of the players seated next to the dealer have lost in the previous deals, the cards are dealt to the next player in rotation. The deal is to the same player as long as he wins for his side, but passes to the next as soon as he loses.

There are certain odds in favour of the dealer at Baccarat (computed to be about $7\frac{1}{2}\%$) and this arises from the fact that the dealer does not make his decision about "drawing" until he has seen the cards drawn by the players. He, of course, knows the conventions and if a player does not draw he therefore knows his point is either 5, 6 or 7. If the player does draw, he knows his point (before the draw) was either 0, 1, 2, 3, 4 or 5, and if there was some hesitation about the matter he can be pretty certain it was 5. He sees the card drawn and can reckon within limits what the player's point now is. Suppose the banker's point is 4, and the punter draws a 9. The latter's point must now be either 9, 0, 1, 2, 3 or 4. It is obvious that the punter has only one chance of winning (i.e. if the point is 9). Thus the banker would "stand" with a considerable prospect of success.

If a player does not draw and the banker's point is 4, he knows he is beaten unless he is fortunate enough to draw a five or under. The odds are against this (8 to 5) and he would not draw unless he was equally badly beaten by the other side of the table. For he has to apply his judgment separately to the two representative players; and where he is certainly beaten on one side, but stands a fair chance on the other he would not draw. The bets on the one side of the table would more or less cover those lost on the other.

Generally a bank finishes automatically when the cards are exhausted, that is when there are less than ten cards left unused.

If the banker retires through "breaking" or otherwise, any punter may continue his bank (i.e. he does not have fresh cards, but takes on those left in the original packs) but he must put either (1) the amount originally put up by the banker if the latter retires "broken", or (2) the amount that the banker takes away; but this amount must equal or exceed the original bank.

The main points to remember are as follows: —

B

A player must not bet out of turn and cannot bet more than the uncovered balance of the bank.

He must not look at his cards until the dealer has announced either a "natural" or "gives".

He must immediately declare a "natural" if he finds he has one.

He must not draw if his point is six or seven.

He must draw if his point is four or under.

He may use his own judgment when the point is five, but the odds are against him.

He must not declare his point, after a draw, until the dealer has declared his.

5. BANKER
(BLIND HOOKEY)

Number of Players: Up to nine players.
Cards: Full pack of 52 cards.

THIS is a game of pure chance. There are various methods of play, but the essence of the game is simply to bet that a card you have received is better than one received or retained by the banker.

The dealer (who is the "banker") is decided by cutting He shuffles the cards and has them cut by the player on his right. He then allows each player to cut a small number of cards (not less than four) from the top of the pack. Those that are left he retains. No player looks at his cards. Each player places a stake beside his cards and the dealer then shows the bottom card of his packet. The other players do the same. The dealer pays out an amount equivalent to their stakes to all who have cards higher than his. All who have cards equal or lower lose their stakes to the dealer. If and when the dealer pays out to all players, the deal passes to the next player and so on.

Instead of allowing each player to cut his own cards, the dealer may cut the pack into three parts. The players choose any two of them and leave the dealer the third. They place their stakes beside one or other of the packets chosen, the cards are turned up and the stakes lost or won as before. The only hint it is necessary to give on playing Banker is: don't play with strangers.

6. BEGGAR MY NEIGHBOUR

Number of Players: Any number.
Cards: Full pack of 52 cards. (If there are more than four persons playing, allow extra packs, i.e. one pack for each four players or portion thereof.)

THIS is one of the simplest of round card games, and one which is entirely suitable for very young children.

The dealer is selected by any conventional method, and he deals an equal number of cards to each player. Any remainder may be set face down in the middle of the table and ignored.

Then, without looking at the cards, the player on the dealer's left turns the top one of his pack and all others do the same in rotation. This turning of cards goes round and round the table, but when a player turns up a court card or an ace, the next player has to pay him a forfeit. This forfeit consists of one card for a jack, two for a queen, three for a king and four for an ace.

If, however, while a forfeit is being paid, one of the above cards happens to be turned the payment is stopped and the player next in turn has to pay a forfeit, according to the scale already indicated, to the one who turned it.

Thus some players are able to win cards and others have to lose them. The aim is to go on winning until one player accumulates the complete pack.

Note that when a person has turned all his cards, he reverses them and without altering their sequence, plays through them again as often as necessary while he remains in the game.

When a player loses all his cards, he falls out; thus the number of players decreases until only one is left, and he obviously is the winner.

7. BOODLE

Number of Players: Up to nine.

Cards: Full pack of 52 cards, plus an additional ace of spades, king of hearts, queen of clubs and jack of diamonds. These last four are known as the "Boodle Cards".

THIS is an excellent game which much resembles Newmarket, but in this instance the betting is simpler.

The four Boodle cards are placed on the table, forming a square, with the ace of spades in the top left hand corner, the king of hearts on its right, the queen of clubs is placed under the ace, and the jack of diamonds goes in the bottom right hand corner, under the king.

Before the cards are dealt, each player puts a counter on each of the four cards on the table. A dealer is selected for the first hand, and thereafter the deal passes in rotation to each player.

The full pack is dealt round to the players, but a dummy hand is provided. The cards belonging to this hand are put in the centre of the table and are never

The four Boodle cards

examined. The dummy cards are dealt as the last hand in each round, as though to an extra player between the dealer and the player on his left. When the game starts, the player on the left of the dealer plays a card. It may be a card of any suit, but it must be the lowest which he holds of that suit. Thereafter, play goes round and round the table; but when a person's turn to play a card comes round, he must either play the card next highest to the previous card or pass. For example suppose that the previous player has played a seven of clubs; if the player immediately on his left does not hold the eight of clubs, he "passes" and the next player has his chance.

A time comes when nobody can go because the king has been reached (kings are high; aces are low in this game) or because the next card happens to be in the dummy hand. This condition is known as a "stop".

Anyone playing a "stop" card has the privilege of laying another card—any he likes so long as it is the lowest he holds of *another* suit, provided he has one—and play then continues from that particular card.

The object of the game is twofold: (a) to be the first to dispose of all the cards in hand and so become the winner of the game, and (b) to hold one of the Boodle cards and to have the opportunity of playing it.

When playing a Boodle card, the player immediately takes all the bets laid on that card. If someone holds a Boodle card and has no chance to play it, or the card is in the dummy hand, the bets are left for the next round and are thus doubled.

The first to get rid of all his cards receives one counter for each card held by all the other players.

Of course the great thing in Boodle is to remember the cards already played, for then it may be possible to play several "stop" cards, one after the other. Naturally a run of cards is helpful when the lead is obtained, because the whole run may then be disposed of.

8. BRAG

Number of Players: Up to eight.
Cards: Full pack of 52 cards.

BRAG has been a favourite for centuries, not only in this
country, but in all parts of the world. Unfortunately, it
is not governed by any definite set of rules; consequently
there are unlimited variations of the game. Here we
describe the method of play which seems to be the most
standard form, without too many additions which might
make play difficult for the uninitiated. In its present
form it may be safely used as a party game; but before
commencing to play it will be wise to read what follows
to the assembled company, in order that all may play on
a common basis.

A dealer is chosen by one of the usual methods and he
deals five cards to each player.

The players then examine their hands and make their
bets in rotation from the dealer's left. The idea is for a
player to bet on the estimated value of his hand in com-
parison with all other existing hands.

The way a hand is assessed varies with different
players, but the following method is much favoured:
Before any bets are made, when the cards have been
examined, the two that are least useful are thrown out.
This leaves a hand which eventually ranks, for the purpose of winning in the following order (it should be
noted here that the word "bragger" applies to either a
nine or jack of any suit):-

1.   Three aces.
2.   Two aces and one bragger.
3.   One ace and two braggers.
4.   Three kings.
5.   Two kings and one bragger.
6.   One king and two braggers.
7.   Three queens.

8. Two queens and one bragger.
9. One queen and two braggers.
10. Three jacks.
11. Two jacks and one nine.
12. One jack and two nines.
13. Three tens.
14. Two tens and one bragger.
15. One ten and two braggers.
16. Three nines.
17. Three eights.
18. Two eights and one bragger, etc., etc., to—
37. One two and two braggers.
38. Two aces.
39. One ace and one bragger.
40. Two kings.
41. One king and one bragger, etc., etc., to—
62. One two and one bragger.

In the above list, No. 1 beats all that follow and all others beat those that follow them. Any combination of cards not mentioned is valueless.

Having set out the rank of the different hands, we will imagine that play is about to begin. The player on the dealer's left has the first bet. He bets whatever he likes (usually up to three counters) that his hand is better than anyone else's. Alternatively, he may bet nothing at all, in which case he drops out.

The first player having bet must place his stake (say three counters) in the pool and those that "come in" after him must each put in a like amount. Then the next player may "come in" on payment of the same stake if he thinks his hand is as good as the first player's.

But the third player may be confident that he holds a better hand; if so, he may "raise" the stakes, saying "I raise it to six counters", i.e. he doubles the first bet. If he does this, he pays six counters into the pool and all who "come in" after him must stake this amount.

This "raising" may cause the fourth, fifth and later players, who perhaps have weak hands, to say "I drop out." The turn thus comes round to the original caller again. If he is still confident that he holds the highest hand, he may say "I raise another three counters", and pays six counters into the pool (three to equalise with the others and three to raise). If, on the other hand, he is not so sure, he may pay three counters to make his stake equivalent to that of the third player. This is called paying "to see". If this happens the betting is at an end. Those who have "come in" and remained in will show their hands and the highest will take the pool.

The two Braggers (All Four Suits)

But the call may go round several times if someone "raises" during each round. Those who wish to remain in the game must make their stakes equivalent to the raiser's or else make a further raise.

At first sight, it may seem that success is a matter of pure chance. This is not so. A good player will keep in mind the probabilities as to whether his hand is likely to have a serious rival according to whether there are few or many players. The number of cards in use will also be taken into account, and he will not fail to study

the behaviour of his opponents. By their demeanour it is
often possible to judge whether their hands are good
or bad.

9. BUBBLY PATIENCE

Number of Players: Up to ten.
Cards: A full pack of cards, per
                        player.

For a crowd of people who enjoy making a noise and
who like something vigorous this is *the* game. It will
entertain any number of players, but about ten is the
limit which we recommend.

Every player is provided with a pack of cards, and
each player must shuffle a pack of cards, other than his
own. The shuffling should be done very thoroughly, in
order to stop the cards getting into runs which would
spoil the fun.

After the shuffling, the players take their packs and do
two things. They deal off the top four cards and set
them, face up, in line before them; then they deal off
the next thirteen cards, which they set in a stack all
facing up, but only the top one showing. This stack
they place near to their right elbow.

So far all the operations have been done leisurely,
but henceforth speed counts. Somebody (previously
selected) says "Are we all ready?" and having been told
"Yes", gives the command "Go". Thereupon the
players dash through the various operations as speedily
as possible.

This is what must be done:

(a) Put any and every ace that comes up, whether in
the line, on the top of the stack or in play, in the centre
of the table.

(b) Build up on the aces in the centre of the table whenever any face-up card allows them to do so. A two goes on an ace, a three on a two, a four on a three, and so on until a king goes on a queen. For this building, it is necessary to keep to the suits. Thus nothing but clubs may go on the ace of clubs, and so with all the other suits.

(c) Build down on the four cards in line. Thus a six goes on a seven, and a ten on a jack; but in this instance one does not have to keep to the suits; instead a red card goes on a black and a black on a red. In other words, the cards have to run in alternate colours.

(d) It must be understood that anybody can build up on any ace formation in the centre of the table, but a player may only build down on his own line formation in front of him.

(e) Play progresses by each player turning his own pack three cards at a time and using the third card whenever it can be played on to some other card. The cards turned up in this way are placed in a stack face up, so that the third card mentioned becomes the top card of this stack.

(f) There is no limit to the number of times a pack may be run through in this way. When the pack has been run through to the end, it is dealt with again and again.

(g) A card exposed by the playing of the third card in a turn up, as in paragraph (e) may also be played in the same manner. Similarly with any other card which subsequently comes to view after the top card has been played, but the order in which the cards appear in the "turn up" stack may not be altered with a view to obtaining a further card which can be played. Only the top card of the stack may be played each time.

(h) Whenever one of the cards or packets in the line formation happens to be used, and a space thus becomes vacant, the space is filled by using the top card from the right-hand stack, which may also be played into any other position as occasion permits.

As soon as somebody has played all his cards on to the suit packs in the centre of the table, he cries "Out" and everyone stops.

It will be readily seen that it is not so much skill as a quick eye and rapid work that enables a player to win.

10. CATCH THE TEN
(Scotch Whist)

Number of Players: Up to eight.

Cards: According to number of players, as follows: —For two three, four or six players, 36 cards from the aces down to sixes of all suits; for five or seven players, as above, with the six of spades removed; for eight players, all cards down to the sevens of all suits (32 cards).

THE cards are dealt in exactly the same way as in *Whist* and play follows the same lines, but the special object of the game is to "catch" or save the ten of trumps, as this adds ten to one's score. Trumps are decided by showing the last card, or by taking the suits in rotation, whichever is previously arranged.

The cards of the non-stop suits have the same values as in *Whist,* but the trump suit ranks in the following order: — *Jack, ace, king, queen, ten, nine, eight, seven and six.*

When play is concluded the following cards take the points shown: jack of trumps=11; ten of trumps=10; ace of trumps=4; king of trumps=3; queen of trumps=2.

In addition, each player counts up the number of cards he has taken in tricks, and from this he deducts the number of cards he was dealt at the outset, and what remains he scores as points. 41 points is game.

There is no definite rule about players and partners. But generally speaking, the best plan is to play individually.

One further point about *Scotch Whist*. It will be seen that the eleven points for the jack of trumps are bound to go to him to whom it is dealt; since it is the highest card in the pack. But the ten points carried by the ten of trumps must be played for, because ace, king and queen of trumps will beat the ten in a trick although their *scoring* value is lower. The great point is to catch the ten, because it makes a difference of 20 points, i.e., ten more for you and ten less for your opponents, or vice versa.

11. CHEAT

Number of Players: Any number.
Cards: Full pack of 52.

THIS is another family game which can be played and enjoyed by younger children.

Each player is given five counters. A pack of cards is shuffled and dealt equally to those taking part in the game. This done, the players look at their cards and sort them out.

When all is ready the player on the dealer's left begins. He puts on the table a card from his hand, face down, and says "One". The player on his left puts down another card and says "Two". The next player follows with a third card saying "Three". In this way the cards mount up until the king is reached, when the cycle reverts to one, and play continues as before, until all the cards are used up, when a new deal is made.

But this is where all the fun comes in. Each player should follow the previous player with a correctly numbered card if he holds one. It may be, however, that he does not hold a card of the number he needs. He must therefore lay down some card and he will put down a wrongly numbered card, announce the right number and try to look innocent, hoping that nobody will take any notice.

At any time when a card is laid, any player may call "Cheat". When this is called, the player setting down the challenged card must expose it. If it is a wrong card, the one who laid it pays the challenger a counter and, if it is a correct card, the one who challenged pays the layer a counter.

The game largely depends on studying the expressions of the players, so it is well to remember that there is such a thing as trying to appear guilty on purpose, in order to win a counter.

12. CHEMIN-DE-FER

Number of Players: Any number.
Cards: Three to six packs.

CHEMIN-DE-FER differs only slightly from Baccarat Banque (which see), but it is rather more popular. The main differences are as under: -

The players are not divided into "sides" against the dealer. One hand only is dealt for the punters and the player betting the largest amount holds it.

The "bank" passes to the next player in rotation every time the banker loses. A banker may, however, at any time withdraw his bank, and in such a case the players in their turns may claim it, if willing to put up as much as is in the bank at the time; or, failing this, it

is auctioned to the highest bidder. When his turn comes
to take the bank a player may refuse if he wishes, and he
is under no obligation as to the amount he must put up
if he takes it. He may risk as much or as little as he likes.

While holding the bank the dealer must, as at
Baccarat, leave all his winnings in—unless the full
amount is not covered by the total bets; in which case
he may withdraw the balance.

The other rules are also as at Baccarat; and as the
holder of the cards is playing for all the money staked
by the punters he is bound by the usual convention to
draw when his point is under five and to stand when it
is six or seven, and may exercise his option when it is
five.

But as the dealer is not playing against two "sides" he
is not allowed by convention to exercise his judgment as
to drawing and is bound to follow a certain recognised
procedure, which is usually set out on a little card as
under: -

If the banker's point is:	And the punter:	The banker must:
0, 1, or 2	Draws any card, or stands	Draw
3, or 4	Draws 10, 9, or 8	Stand
	Draws 7, 6, 5, 4, 3, 2, or 1 or stands	Draw
5	Draws 10, 9, 8, 2 or 1	Stand
	Draws 7, 6, 5, 4, 3, or stands	Draw
6	Draws 6 or 5	Draw
	Draws 10, 9, 8, 7, 4, 3, 2, or 1 or stands	Stand
7	Draws any card or stands	Stand
8 or 9		Declare natural.

By reason of this convention, the odds are not nearly
so much in the banker's favour as at Baccarat.

The secret of the game's popularity lies probably in
the fact that every player gets a turn as banker, and there
is no need for him to risk any more than he can well
afford. There is no doubt that it is more exciting to be
banker, although it is not quite clear why. The turn

comes round fairly quickly and thus a player who loses his bank at the first deal is not discouraged.

It is sometimes agreed that a banker who has had three wins in succession may withdraw from the bank a half of his winnings (not half the whole bank) and where this rule is observed it adds a certain zest.

Whilst waiting for his turn as banker, a player must of course bet—at least on every third deal. Any player who attempted to do the majority of his gambling as banker could be called on to "retire".

13. COMBINE

Number of Players: Any number.
Cards: Two full packs (with different backs)

THIS is an easy game to learn, as the rules are few and simple. The dealer is selected by the usual method and takes one of the packs, which he deals round the table; then he turns to the second pack and deals it round in the same manner. When he has finished, everybody has two equal stacks of cards, both face down.

The deal being completed the combining is undertaken. To do this, each player uses both hands and lifts a card from both stacks simultaneously, placing the left card under the right, thus forming a new and larger stack. When the two piles have been incorporated into one stack, a glance at the patterns on the back of the cards will show immediately whether the combining has been done correctly. If two similar backs show together anywhere in a player's new stack, it is the dealer's duty to cancel the hand at once, since such a condition shows that the combining is faulty.

When all the backs have been suitably checked, the

dealer knocks on the table and each person turns his cards, without altering the sequence, and looks at them for the first time.

(a) When two adjoining cards make a pair of the same value, they count one point.

(b) When three adjoining cards make a pair-royal (three of the same value), they count three points.

(c) When four adjoining cards make a double pair-royal (four of the same value) they count six points.

(d) Three adjoining cards of the same suit count one point.

31 points is game.

14. COME SEVEN

Number of Players: Any number.
Cards: An ordinary pack, less aces and kings. Allow at least five cards per person, and use two or more packs, as necessary.

THE cards should be dealt round to each player in the normal way, and everyone participating in the game should be asked to contribute one counter to the pool.

After the deal, the player on the dealer's left takes a dice cup, shakes up two dice and throws them. According to the total number of the pips shown on the face of the two dice, so the player looks at his hand to see whether he has a card therein of equal value. That is to say, if the dice thrown show a two and one, the player will play a three of any suit from his hand, provided he holds such a card. All numeral cards are assessed at their face value, with a jack counting 11 and a queen, 12. When seven is thrown on the dice and is matched by a card, the player in question takes one counter from the pool.

C

A player who is able to throw out a card has another turn with the dice and continues to do so, until he no longer holds a card to match the dice. A player who cannot match the dice, hands the cup to his neighbour on the left and the game proceeds. In this way the game continues, until one player has disposed of all his cards. The player doing this takes whatever remains in the pool.

15. COMMERCE

Number of Players: Any number.
Cards: Full pack of 52 cards.

COMMERCE is a game belonging to the *Poker* family, but unlike that game is easily learnt.

A dealer is selected in the usual way and deals out three cards to each player. Before looking at their cards, the players contribute an agreed number of counters to the pool. Two each is a practical number when no more than five play, while one is sufficient when the party is large.

The object of a player is to get by trade or barter a series of three cards alike, a sequence of three cards or what is known as a point.

(a)   Three cards alike means three cards of the same rank but of different suits, such as three aces or three tens.

(b)   A sequence is three cards of the same suit with consecutive values such as four, five and six of spades.

(c)   A point consists of two or three cards of the same suit which show a higher number of pips than a similar combination in any other hand. For this purpose, aces count as eleven and all court cards count ten.

These are the series of cards which have a counting value and no other combinations count anything. Any series of three cards beats any sequence and any sequence beats any point. In addition, a high series will beat a low series, and the same applies to sequences and points.

To explain the latter statement, the best hand to hold is three aces, the next best three kings, then three queens and so on. Three twos are the worst trio to hold, but even so they are better than the best sequence which is ace, king and queen of the same suit. The worst sequence is the three, two and ace of a suit. Note that an ace, here, can be high or low.

The best cards to hold for Commerce (Any 3 Aces)

In the same way the worst sequence is better than the best point combination. Point combinations depend on the total pip values of the cards held, but the cards must be of the same suits. In the case of a tie, the total which is made by three cards of the same suit beats the same total made by only two cards.

At the outset we spoke of trade and barter. Trading consists of paying a counter to the dealer, who keeps it, in exchange for the top unknown card of the remainder pack. At the time of receiving this card, the player throws out his least useful card, face down. No player ever has more than three cards in his hand at a time.

Barter consists in exchanging a card with a neighbour sitting on the left. Of course bartering is done "blind", i.e. the giver and receiver must not know what each other wants.

As soon as anybody is satisfied with his cards, he knocks; the game stops and all the hands are assessed. The game also stops when anyone refuses to barter with his neighbour. The highest hand, as reckoned by the rules already explained, takes the pool.

For the next game, the player sitting on the last dealer's left becomes the new dealer. Note that trading and bartering are done in order round and round the table.

16. COON-CAN

Number of Players: Up to six.
Cards: Two packs of 52 cards plus one joker.

THIS is a game of the *Rummy* family. The two packs of cards and the joker are all shuffled well together.

After cutting for dealer, the cards are dealt out one by one to each player, until everyone holds ten cards. The remainder of the pack is laid face down in the centre of the table, and the uppermost card is placed face upwards alongside the pack.

The object of the game is for each player to get rid of all his cards by laying out on the table pair-royals or running flushes of three cards. (A pair-royal is three cards of the same rank—e.g. three sixes; a running-flush is three cards of the same suit in numerical order, e.g. six, seven and eight of clubs).

The player on the dealer's left plays first. He picks up either the faced-up card or the unexposed card from the top of the pack, whichever he pleases. Having done this, he may lay out any pair-royals or running flushes he now holds. If he cannot, or does not wish to do this, he must throw out one of his cards to replace the card he has drawn, placing it face upwards beside the pack.

The next player now draws a card, lays out, and/or discards, as the case may be, and so on for all the other players.

When once some cards have been laid out by a player those that follow him may, between drawing and discarding, add any cards from their hands to the combination on the table, no matter who laid them out.

Thus if there are, say, three sevens on the table, and a player holds a seven, he may add it to the three already laid. Or if there is a sequence of, say, five, six and seven of hearts on the table, and a player holds the four and eight of hearts he may use these to add to the sequence at both ends.

The joker of course may be made to represent any card. If it is laid out at the end of the sequence, a player wishing to add to that sequence may move it to the other end if it suits him. For instance, if a player has laid down a six, seven and joker (representing eight), a player wishing to add the three and four could move the joker to the other end of the sequence, making it the five. He could then add his three and four, making the run of three, four, joker (five), six and seven. The joker can be moved once only, however, and if it is originally placed in the middle of a sequence it cannot be moved at all. Once moved, from one end of a sequence to the other, the joker is "fixed" to indicate that this has been done. To "fix" the joker, simply means that it is laid crossways to the run of cards.

Aces may count high or low in a running flush of one-two-three or ace-king-queen. Note, however, that king-one-two is not a run.

As soon as a player gets rid of all his cards the hand is at an end. The others show the cards they still hold and pay him one stake for each "pip". The joker counts 15, the ace 11 and all court cards as ten; the rest of the cards count at face value.

If no player gets "out" before the pack is exhausted the drawing must then all be done from the top of the discard pile; and the players *must* discard a *different* card every time. Previously, they were at liberty to discard the same card as they drew, if they so wished.

A typical Coon-can "run" using the Joker as the three or six of Clubs

Certain simple principles should be borne in mind when playing. If you cannot secure cards to make the desired combinations, you can at least reduce the "count" of your hand by discarding your high cards. The joker is to some extent a dangerous card to hold, since it counts 15 against you, but it can generally be used pretty soon, so you should hold it for a hand or two.

By observation of the cards being drawn by other players (that is, if they are drawing from the discard pile), it may be possible to assess what they are trying to play. If you see a player happily grabbing a king from the discard pile, then you might judge that he is "collecting" kings, and in this case you would refrain from discarding a king if you possibly could.

Similarly, watch all discards. It is of no use hanging on to two queens, if two have already been thrown out on the discard pile, where there is practically no hope of getting them.

But the chief opportunity for the display of skill is in choosing the moment to "lay out". It is obvious that the sooner you lay out the sooner you give your opponents the chance of "adding". Hence it may be wise to hold your complete combinations for a while—but not too long, or someone else may suddenly lay down his entire hand and call upon you for stakes according to your "count".

17. DO OR DIE

Number of Players: Five to ten players.
Cards: Full pack of 52 cards.

THE cards are dealt out according to the number of people playing thus:

```
5  players—10 cards each and 2 on the table
6  players— 8 cards each and 4 on the table
7  players— 7 cards each and 3 on the table
8  players— 6 cards each and 4 on the table
9  players— 5 cards each and 7 on the table
10 players— 5 cards each and 2 on the table.
```

The cards laid on the table are placed singly and face up so that anyone can use them when it helps to do so. All other cards are dealt face down and must remain so until the time comes to turn them.

Each player has his stack of cards on the table in front of him. Then the player on the dealer's left turns his top card and places it face up on the table, where it can be seen by all. Subsequent players do likewise in rotation. After the first round, a turned card which cannot be played elsewhere must be set on top of the card which the player previously turned.

The aim of each player is to get rid of his cards as quickly as possible by playing them on to the faced cards of other players in descending order and in alternate colours. Thus the sequence is red ace, black king, red queen, etc. When the ace (as one) is again reached, the king follows and there is no stop to the sequence.

Suppose for instance the turn to play reaches A. The top card of his faced packet is a three of diamonds and he sees that the top card of B's faced packet is a four of spades. He puts his three on the four and thus rids his hand of one card. After that the turn passes to the next player.

But, suppose again, A had no faced card that would fit anywhere. In such a case he would turn up the next card on his non-faced stack, hoping that it might fit somewhere. Remember, however, that he may not handle more than one of his cards during the same turn.

The faced cards on the table are used in the following manner. A has, say, a faced three of diamonds, another player has a faced five of hearts and amongst the cards in the centre of the table there is a four of spades; A is then able to play the four on to the five and the three on to the four, thereby getting rid of his faced card.

The player having disposed of all his cards first wins the game.

18. DUTCH BANK

Number of Players: Up to 12, seven or eight
make the best company.
Cards: Ordinary pack of 52 cards.

BEFORE play commences a banker is selected, by means of cutting. The person cutting the lowest card (ace low) takes the bank.

Next, each player is given an agreed number of counters—say, thirty which is a reasonable amount.

The banker shuffles the cards which are then cut by the person sitting on the banker's left.

The banker holding the cards face downwards, then drops cards from the bottom of the pack on to the table, thus making a packet for each player. It does not matter how many cards go to a packet and each packet may be made up of a different number. The only requisite is that each pack must consist of a minimum of four cards.

The players then each reach forward and appropriate a packet each but they do not lift the packets up, they slide them along to where they are sitting. The banker may not select, he has to take whichever packet is left.

Now the banker turns up his top card and other players do likewise. The banker pays a counter to every person whose top card is of greater value than his, and collects a counter from all the players whose top card is equal to or smaller than his. King is reckoned highest, ace lowest.

The cards are all thrown in, the pack is remade and the person on the dealer's left, becomes the new banker and the game is repeated.

19. FARO

Number of Players: Any number.
Cards: A complete pack of 52 cards,
                        plus the complete suit of
                        spades taken from another
                        pack.

FARO has rather a bad name amongst card players, but in actual fact its reputation is unmerited, it being no better and no worse than any other game of chance where a degree of skill is needed.

First of all, lay out the suit of spades on the table, as follows:

King   Queen Jack   Ten   Nine Eight
                                            Seven
Ace   Two   Three   Four   Five   Six

If preferred, it is possible to purchase a proper Faro lay-out cloth, on which is painted these thirteen cards.

A banker is then elected and whoever takes on the office continues in the post until the whole pack is exhausted; then someone else takes his place.

The pack is shuffled, cut and set on the table with all the cards faced up. The top card alone can be seen. All is now ready for the bets. Each punter puts two counters on any of the cards in the lay-out.

The bets having been staked, the banker throws off the top card of the pack and, in that way, exposes another card. That belongs to him, and he thereupon collects all the counters which may be touching the card of similar value shown on the "lay-out". It need not be of the same suit; in Faro, no notice whatsoever is taken of suit, it is the face value of a card only which counts.

Thus if, say, a six of diamonds comes up, the banker wins all the counters placed on the six of spades in the lay-out.

Next the banker throws off his card and exposes

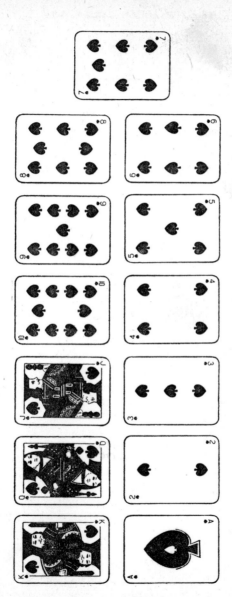

The lay-out for Faro

another. This is the punters' card. The banker then pays out "evens" to all who have put their bets on this particular card. Here again, it must be remembered that it is only the rank and not the suit that counts.

These two cards make a "turn" and, when the bets on them have been attended to, the "turn" is finished. Punters who have staked on other cards pick up their counters and a fresh "turn" commences. Note particularly, however, that the pack is not rearranged. It is used for "turn" after "turn" until no more cards are left.

On the fact that the pack is not reshuffled between the turns depends much of the skill of the game. Each punter makes a list of the cards that have gone and bets on the probabilities of those that are to come.

It should be remarked, in conclusion, that when the two cards of a turn form a pair, the banker takes half the stakes.

In some circles a much more complicated game of Faro is played, but the version given here is the most popular and simplest form of the game.

20. FOUR JACKS

Number of Players: Up to seven.
Cards: Pack of 32 cards consisting of all four aces, kings, queens, jacks, tens, nines, eights and sevens. (When five or six players are in the game the two black sevens are also thrown out.

THIS is a lively game for those who know how to play *Whist*. When seven persons sit down, the usual plan is for the dealer to pass his hand.

The jacks of hearts, clubs or diamonds count one point each against the holder. The jack of spades counts two points

Cutting, dealing and otherwise handling the cards calls for no particular comment, but each player must have the same number of cards. When the number of players makes this impossible, the joker is added to the pack and in this case, the joker ranks as the highest card of all. It is, in fact, the "super-trump" card.

Play is directed towards making tricks, exactly as is done in *Whist*. Suits led must be followed wherever possible, trumps may only be played when no card of the led suit is held, and so on, but there is an essential difference. A player must try to take no trick with a jack in it. At the end of a game the tricks held are not counted; only the jacks in the tricks are important and these are counted *against* the holder (Two for the jack of spades, one for each other jack).

Each player plays for himself, not as a partner, and he starts to play with ten points. The first to lose all his ten points pays each of the others according to the number of points they still have in hand.

21. GAIGEL

Number of Players: Up to eight.
Cards: Pack of forty-eight consisting of the ace, king, queen, jack, ten and seven of all four suits taken from two packs. Thus there are two cards of every kind.

THIS is another game of the *Whist* variety, but in this instance play is individual and not in partnership.

Each player is given five cards by the dealer, three at a time and then two. The object of the game is not to make the highest number of tricks, but to make tricks

A Double Common Marriage for Gaigel = 40 points.
If Spades were Trumps, this would then rank as a
Double Royal Marriage = 80 points

that contain certain cards. Points are given for these cards and the one who first reaches a score of 101 is the winner.

The method of playing, unless anything is stated here to the contrary, is the same as for *Whist*. For instance, the highest card laid wins a trick and trumps rank before the suit led; but there is no rule about following suit. Trumps are determined by the turn up, which is the next card on the pack after the deal is finished.

One curious rule in the game is that, when a trick is finished, each player takes a card from the remnant pack, beginning with the winner of the trick who appropriates the top face-down card.

This taking of an extra card maintains the hands at their original number; but it can only last while there is any part of the pack left. As soon as this is exhausted, a different set of rules comes into force. A player must then follow suit if he can, and must play a higher card than any laid if he holds one.

Note that, throughout, when two similar cards happen to be played in the same trick, the first one takes precedence.

When a game is finished the cards are scrutinised and each player takes the following points for any of the combinations indicated which he may be able to get together.

(a) Common Marriage (king and queen of the same non-trump suit)   Score— 20

(b) Double Common Marriage (two sets as above)
                                                      Score— 40

(c) Royal Marriage (king and queen of the trump suit)   Score— 40

(d) Double Royal Marriage (two sets as above)
                                                      Score— 80

(e) Five sevens (held in the hand or won in tricks at any moment of the game)   Score—101

(f) Every ace won in tricks   Score— 11

(g) Every ten won in tricks   Score— 10

(h) Every king won in tricks   Score— 4
(i) Every queen won in tricks   Score— 3
(j) Every jack won in tricks   Score— 2

Note that items (a) to (e) may be made up of cards dealt in the hand, as well as those won in tricks. It is, of course, not sufficient to have held certain cards and to have played them into a lost trick.

22. HIGH CARD POOL

Number of Players: Up to eight.
Cards: Normal pack of 52.

THIS is a lively game which requires each player to have about 30 counters. In this game suits are disregarded.

Before starting the actual play each player draws a card from the pack. The one to get the lowest card deals. The next lowest sits on his left and all others take their seats in rotation. Then each puts one counter into the pool or, if fewer than five people are playing, it is advisable to contribute two counters.

Following these preliminaries, the dealer gives out five cards to each player and places the remainder pack face down on the table.

It is now the turn of the player on the left of the dealer to make his bet. He scrutinises his hand and does one of two things. Either he passes (this requires him to pay a counter into the pool) or he says "I bet (so many) counters that I can beat the turn up". He may bet any number he likes, as long as it does not exceed the counters in the pool.

His bet being made, the top card of the pack is turned. If he can beat it, he lays the one card necessary to beat it and no others. Then he takes from the pool as many counters as he bet. But if he cannot beat it he shows no

D

cards and puts an amount equivalent to his bet in the pool.

It is is important to note that players waiting their turn must not show their cards to others. Also, the one who is actually betting must show no more than the one card needed to prove his bet. These regulations are imperative because it would be helpful to those waiting their turn to know of the whereabouts of as many as possible.

Ace, in this game, counts high; and whenever the pool is exhausted each player puts in the required counter or counters to replenish it. The one who happened to empty it is not excused from this.

23. I DOUBT IT

Number of Players: Any number.
Cards: The necessary number of full packs of 52 cards to enable each player to have six-eight cards with five or six cards left over.

THE cards should be dealt equally to each player, with the remaining five or six left on the table.

When each player has sorted out his cards, the player on the dealer's left takes three cards from his hand, and placing these face downwards on the table says to the player sitting on his left, "These are three queens," or three anything else. That player then weighs up the situation and says "Oh" or "I doubt it." If he says the former it means that he is not prepared to contest the statement and the one who laid them is entitled to place the three cards on the remainder pack. Nobody is allowed to see whether they were three queens or not. If, however, the player approached says "I doubt it" the cards in question are immediately turned for scrutiny.

If his original statement is not true, the player who laid the cards has to pick these up and take into his hand any cards that, at the moment are on the table. If the statement is true, the doubter has to take up the three cards concerned and all the tabled cards.

When the first three cards have been settled, the second player does exactly the same thing as the first; but he may call three of anything, not necessarily what was originally called. In this way the play continues round and round the table until, at last, someone wins the game by getting rid of all his cards.

If a player finds himself with fewer than three cards he must make these up to three by picking at random one or more cards from the table, and if there happen to be no cards on the table at the moment, he must wait until there are.

24. LANSQUENET

Number of Players: Any number.
Cards: Full pack of 52.

THIS game is very easy to learn and, though simple, it provides plenty of thrills. One player is selected as banker, and the others play as punters.

The cards must be thoroughly shuffled and cut, following which the banker turns up two top cards and places these side by side on the table. These are called the "hand" cards. Next he deals one card for himself below the hand cards and another for the company above the hand cards. The latter is known as the *réjouissance* card. Should there be any duplicates in these four cards, they are placed one on top of the other and the spaces thus created are filled with fresh cards from the top of the pack. The reason for this is that all four cards—the two hand cards, the banker's card and the réjouissance card—must be of different values.

The backers now make their bets, placing whatever sums they like against the réjouissance card. The banker replies by staking like amounts against each bet and then turns up the top card from the remaining pack.

If this card is of the same value as the réjouissance card the banker wins all bets and recovers his stake; if it is similar to his own card each backer recovers his bet and receives a like sum from the banker's stake; if it is similar to one of the hand cards, it is put to cover that card and the next card from the pack is turned up; but if it is not like any of the cards on the table it is placed by the side of the réjouissance card and further bets may be laid against it before the next card from the pack is turned.

If any backers bet against the additional réjouissance cards, the banker must offset such bets with like amounts.

When any one of the betting cards is matched the stakes remaining against the unmatched réjouissance cards are reclaimed by the backers and banker respectively; the cards are shuffled and cut and a fresh game is commenced.

At this stage the bank may be passed to another player if desired, but it is usual for one player to hold the bank for six games.

It will be seen from the above explanation that suits do not count in Lansquenet; only the face value of the card matters.

25. LOO

Number of Players: Four to ten.
Cards: Full pack of 52.

THIS is a very old game and one much beloved of the inveterate card-playing ladies of the eighteenth century. There are many versions, but that described here is the most popular and the simplest method of play.

The dealer is selected in the usual manner, and every player places one counter in the pool. The cards are dealt singly round the table until each player has received three cards, and a dummy hand of three cards known as the "Miss", is also dealt. The next card on the remaining pack is then turned up for trumps.

The players having looked at their cards, the player on the immediate left is asked by the dealer what he intends to do. This player may play the hand he holds, change it for the Miss, or he may throw in his hand for the round.

If the first player does not take the Miss, the next player on the left is given the option and if he likewise refuses the offer is passed round until it is taken or everybody has refused.

When somebody has taken the Miss, the remaining players have the choice of either playing or throwing in their hand. Naturally if a hand is thrown in, it means that the player is out of the game for that round.

No hand thrown in or exchanged for the Miss may be examined by the other players.

Should a player take the Miss and all other players throw in their hands, that player takes the whole of the pool without having to play for it. If one player only elects to play, but has refused the Miss, the dealer must play him with either his own or the dummy hand. If everybody throws in their hands, the dealer takes the pool.

The preliminary decisions having been made, the first player on the dealer's left who has elected to play, commences. His aim and that of the other players is to win tricks as in *Whist,* but he must play according to these rules and not as he chooses.

(a) If he has two trumps in hand, he must play one of them.

(b) If only two people have decided to play and the leader has either two or three trumps, he must play the highest of them. But if he has two consecutive trumps, he may play either; if he has three consecutive trumps, he may play any one of them. Also, if his trumps and the turn-up are consecutive, he again may play any of them.

(c) If he holds the ace of trumps, he must play it.

(d) If the ace of trumps is the turn-up and he holds the king, he must play it.

The leader having played, subsequent players must:

(a) Follow the suit where they can.

(b) Play a trump, if they hold one, when they cannot follow suit.

(c) Play a higher card than any laid, if they are able.

The winner of a trick, leads the next round and he is bound by the rules already set out but, in addition, if he holds at least one trump, he must play it as his lead.

When the three tricks have been made, the pool is divided into three and a third goes to the winner of each trick. Odd counters that cannot be shared are left to swell the next pool and the deal passes to the left.

Players who have won no tricks are "looed"; i.e., they have to pay into the next pool two counters instead of one.

26. MISS MILLIGAN'S AUNT

Number of players: Any number.
Cards: Two full packs of 52 cards
                        each.

THE two packs of cards are shuffled well together and a
dealer is selected, who makes the pack and lays out the
first eight cards face up in line. Then he gives five cards
to each of the players, dealing the cards singly.

The hands are examined and play passes in turn to
the left around the table. The idea is to build cards
downwards and in alternate colours on the eight cards
ranged in line on the table, one card being played at
each turn.

Thus on a red six a player may put a black five, or on
a black ten, a red nine may be placed. A player
may also join up two rows of cards. For instance if, say,
there is one pile made up of a red ten, black nine, red
eight and black seven; and another pile made up of a
black five, red four and black three, the player may
combine the two by playing the red six on to the first
pile and adding the second pile on to it. When such an
event takes place the player responsible for the combining may put any card he likes from his hand to start
a new pile in the vacant space.

When his turn comes and a player has no card in his
hand to add to the eight piles in the centre, he must
draw from the remainder pack until a suitable card is
found, or if the pack has been exhausted, he must pass.

It should be noted that there is no "stop" to a pile
when an ace is reached, play continues by placing a king
of the opposite colour on to the ace.

The player first disposing of all his cards receives a
counter from each other player.

A game of Miss Milligan's Aunt in progress

27. MONTE BANK

Number of players: Any number.
Cards: Forty cards, comprising a full pack less all the eights, nines and tens.

FOR people who like a good speculative game without a lot of complicated thinking, this is first rate.

A banker is chosen, and this office is held by different players after each set of eight bets—i.e., when he has turned up all the cards in his pack, which will be explained later. The bank is normally passed around the table in much the same way as the deal would be.

When play starts, the banker holds the pack and puts the two top cards from it on the table, face up and side by side. Then he does the same to the two bottom cards. The four cards should form a rectangle of two rows of two cards; the upper row coming from the top of the pack, the lower row from the bottom.

The lay-out being completed, each player (except the banker) puts a counter on the upper edge or the lower edge of the rectangle as he thinks fit. Then when all the bets are made, the banker slides off the bottom card from the pack and exposes it. This is known as the "gate".

If the gate belongs to the same suit as either of the upper cards the banker pays one counter each to those who bet on the upper edge of the rectangle, and those backers take up their stakes, while the bets on the lower edge are appropriated by the banker.

If the gate belongs to the same suit as either of the lower cards, a similar course is followed in that those backers who have bet on the lower edge of the rectangle receive their own stakes back, plus one counter from the banker. Those laid on the top part are taken by the banker.

If the gate belongs to a suit unrepresented in either line, the banker takes up all the money laid.

The five used cards are then placed aside and the next lay-out and gate cards are drawn from the pack in the same manner. In this way play continues until the pack is exhausted when the cards are reshuffled and the bank changes hands.

28. NAP

Number of Players:	Upwards of three players (three to six persons for preference).
Cards:	Full pack of 52 cards.

THIS game, a great favourite, is a splendid introduction to the more complex game of *Contract Bridge*. It is a game, however, that should never be played for money with strangers as the opportunities for false deals and other irregularities are innumerable.

Nap is usually played for so much a trick and the cards rank as for *Whist*, ace highest and two lowest. The deal is determined by turning up one card in front of each player—the lowest card turned up taking the deal. In assessing the value for deal, ace counts low. The cards are shuffled by the player on the dealer's left and cut by the player on the dealer's right, and the cards are then dealt singly round the table until each player has received five cards.

The undealt cards must be placed in a heap face downwards in the middle of the table and these are not touched again until the round is over, except at Purchase Nap, when the dealer retains possession of the pack until the purchases have been effected.

The object of each player is to win as many tricks as he

can. Since only five cards are dealt to each, five is obviously the highest number of tricks that can be won (or "made") in one hand.

The first move in the game is the process of "calling". The eldest hand (he who sits on the left of the dealer) has the first call. He states how many tricks he thinks he can win, with all the other players against him. The rest of the players, each in his turn from left to right, now have the option of making a higher call, or of saying "pass" which means they cannot do better than the previous caller. Thus it will be seen that the dealer always has the last call. The lowest permissible call is three. The highest call is Nap—which means that the player undertakes to win all five tricks. Because this is difficult to do the player is allowed odds of two to one. That is, if he makes Nap he is paid by each player twice the stake for each trick.

When everyone has called, the play begins. The highest caller has the lead, and the first card he plays (face upwards on the table before him) determines the trump suit for the hand. Hence it will be seen that in deciding what to call, a player is guided by the fact that he can make his own trumps. The game then follows the general rules as laid down for *Whist*—i.e. a player must follow suit where he can, and, if such is not possible, trump or throw away, according to his hand and the run of the game. It must be remembered that, at Nap, there are no partners as such. The person making the highest call plays alone in his endeavour to make good his call, whilst the other players play together to try and prevent him from making the stated number of tricks. If the highest bidder fails to make good his claim, he must pay one counter (two counters if a Nap hand was called) to each of the other players. On the other hand, should he complete the requisite number of tricks he collects one counter from each player, or two counters if he has called and made a Nap hand. It should be noted, however, that if three or four tricks were called the player only receives one counter from each player, even if he has succeeded in winning all five tricks. In other words, he may only receive the double payment for a Nap hand, if he originally made that call. Among some devotees of Napoleon Whist, the call *Misère* is permitted. This means that the player guarantees to make no tricks at all, in which instance of course, all the other players combine to try to make him win a trick. Playing to lose, in such circumstances, is just as difficult as playing to win, but should the player calling "misère" succeed in taking no tricks at all, he receives the same payment as he would for a "three" or "four" hand. The misère call ranks higher than the three or four call, but lower than the Nap bid.

Purchase Nap, mentioned above, is a more complex variation of the game. It is played in this fashion. After all the players have inspected the dealt hands and before calling commences, the dealer asks each player in turn if he wishes to "buy". A player may buy any number of cards up to five—paying one counter for *each* card. In exchange for each card bought he must throw out one from his original hand, without showing it, of course. These discards are not used again until the next hand, and cards cannot be exchanged more than once. The pool thus created in Purchase Nap goes to the first player who calls and successfully makes Nap.

29. NEWMARKET

Number of players: Three or more.
Cards: Ordinary pack of 52 cards.

BEFORE the deal is made the four aces are removed from the pack and placed face upwards in the centre of the table. Each player then makes his "bet" by placing a counter on whichever of the aces he chooses, and pays another counter into the pool. The dealer having been chosen, the cards are then dealt round, one at a time, to each player, and a dummy hand dealt in the centre of the table. This dummy hand may be taken in exchange by any player, the dealer having the first option and the choice being passed in turn clockwise around the table. If the dealer wishes to change his hand for the dummy he may do so without payment, but if any other player chooses to exercise his option he must pay one counter into the pool. Once the dummy hand is taken up, no further exchanges may be made.

Play is continued by the person on the immediate left of the dealer laying his lowest *red* card, say, the three of hearts. The player holding the four of hearts plays it, followed by the five, six and so on until the "stop" is reached. The stop occurs when the next card in the sequence is held in the dummy hand and thus cannot be played. The person playing the stop card, continues with his lowest card in the opposite coloured suits. That is to say, in the instance above where the three, four, five and six of hearts have been played, let us suppose that the seven is in the dummy hand and cannot therefore be played. The six thus becomes the stop card and the player who laid the six continues to play by playing his lowest *black* card. Play continues in this fashion on alternate black and red suits until one player has exhausted his hand. If the player laying the stop card is unable to lay another card of the alternate coloured suit, the chance to do so is passed to the player on his left and, if he cannot, the option passes round to the left until one player can do so. Should all the cards of one colour have been laid, the chance reverts to the original player who laid the stop card, who proceeds to play the lowest card in his hand.

When any player lays the king of a suit he takes all the counters which have been placed on the ace of that particular suit. The person first to clear his entire hand takes whatever counters are in the pool and the round

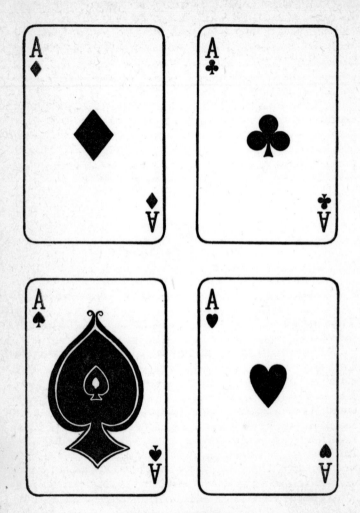

The four Newmarket cards

is then finished, irrespective of what cards may be held by other players. Should any counters be left on any of the aces at the end of a hand, due to the fact that the king has not been played, these are left there during subsequent hands, until the necessary king *has* been played. The deal passes round in turn, each time to the player on the left of the previous dealer.

As will be seen this is a game of more or less pure chance. In backing a particular ace, the player follows his own whim and fancy, and the order of play of cards is dictated by the sequence. The only time when a player may perhaps help his luck along is by choosing the dummy hand in exchange for his dealt hand.

30. OLD MAID

Number of players: Up to nine.
Cards: Full pack of 52 cards.

THIS game, an old nursery favourite, is particularly enjoyed by the very young, as well as by their elders.

The queen of spades is removed from the pack which is then dealt round, one card at a time, to the players. The cards are examined and each player discards any pairs (i.e. two fives, two sixes, etc.) which he may hold in his hand. This done, the player on the dealer's left offers his hand, spread fan-wise backs uppermost, to his left-hand neighbour who must take one card. If this pairs with one card which he holds, he throws out the pair. If it does not, he adds the card to his hand; which is, in turn, offered in the same way to the next person on the left. This goes on until all players have managed to clear their hands by "pairing"— all that is except the unfortunate player left holding the odd queen. He, or she, is the "Old Maid" and must pay a suitable forfeit.

31. PATIENCE POKER

Number of Players: Any number.
Cards: One full pack per player
                           (preferably, these packs
                           should be of the small
                           patience size since the lay-
                           out of the cards takes up a
                           lot of room on the table).

ONE player is elected to be the "caller", and the caller
shuffles his pack of cards and lays it face downwards in
front of him. The other players put their packs of cards
into numerical order of each suit.

The caller announces twenty-five cards, one at a time,
selected by turning the card on the top of his pack face
upwards, and each player must place the corresponding
card from his hand, in the form of a rectangle on the
table in front of him—five cards across, five cards down.
The rectangle is obviously built up gradually and is
only complete when the twenty-fifth card is named.
While it is being built, a player is free to put any card
in any of the spaces that are empty as long as a card, on
being laid, touches some previous card at the top, side or
corner. Obviously, an exception is made in the case of
the first card, which may go anywhere. Each card must be
laid as the caller names it, or certainly before he names
the next card. Once any particular card has been placed
it must not be moved. The caller also builds up his own
rectangle from the cards as he turns each one from the
pack in front of him.

When the rectangles are complete, each player reckons
up the scores which can be made from their own arrange-
ments.

The score is counted by points, thus:

(a)   A straight flush (five consecutive cards of the same
       suit in a line)   counts 30 points

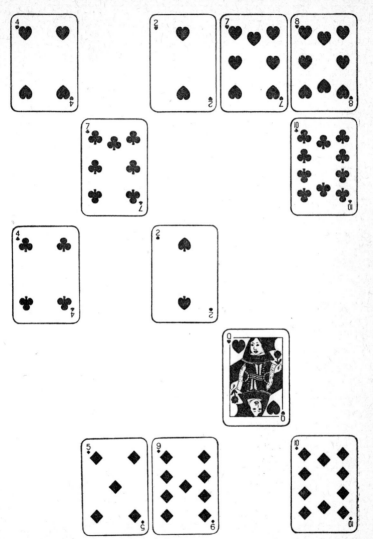

The plan of a game of Patience Poker in progress

(b)   Four cards of the same rank in a line

counts 16 points

(c)   A straight (five consecutive cards, not of the same suit in a line)   counts 12 points

(d)   A full house (three cards of the same rank and two of another in a line)   counts 10 points

(e)   Three of a kind, and two other cards not a pair

counts 6 points

(f)   A flush (five cards of the same suit but not consecutive in a line)   counts 5 points

(g)   Two pairs in a line   counts 3 points

(h)   One pair in a line   counts 1 point

The count can be made along a row or along a column, thus it will be seen that a quick brain is needed to ensure that the 25 called cards are placed to the best advantage. A rubber is five games and the winner is he who has scored the highest number of points after the completion of the fifth game.

32. PELMANISM

Number of Players: Any number.
Cards: Full pack of 52.

PELMANISM is also known as the "Memory Game", and is particularly enjoyed by children.

The cards are spread out, backs uppermost, on the table—in a haphazard fashion, and not regularly arranged.

Each player takes it in turn to lift any two of the cards, show them and replace them in the same position. If, however, the cards are a pair, the player removes them to a heap in front of him, and they count as a trick to him.

The essence of the game lies in remembering where

particular cards are, so that when you raise your first card, it is easy to go for its fellow and thus secure a "pair".

At the beginning it may be easy to remember where three or four of the cards have been placed, but as the game proceeds, one is apt to get a little mixed.

The winner is obviously he who secures the largest number of tricks.

33. PLAYING THE RACES

Number of Players: Any number.
Cards: Full pack of 52.

THIS exciting game is one of pure chance. Before the game begins, each player is given a number of tokens, say 500, which are made up of various colours. White counts one, red counts five, blue counts twenty-five and yellow counts a hundred. Each player should receive the same number of tokens made up of all colours, and totalling the same amount. One of the players is then chosen to act as banker.

The next requirement is a large sheet of paper on which to draw out the "course", which is shown on the following page.

When play is about to start, each punter makes a bet either on red or black, or on a particular column. Counters placed above the word "red" or "black" are even bets on the colour selected, while bets on a particular column are placed just above the selected column, the odds for these being five to one.

The counters having been laid, the banker takes two complete packs of cards, shuffles them together and has them cut by another player. He throws off the top card and deals the next six cards, one each to the crosses on the "course".

When the six cards are laid the banker takes the highest among them (ace is high, two is low), and advances this card to the line above. That done he lays six more cards on the crosses and, in the same way advances the highest card. When a column has already earned one advance and is fortunate in getting another, the top card in it is advanced to the second line and so on, as the game proceeds.

	RED			BLACK	
—	—	—	—	—	—
—	—	—	—	—	—
—	—	—	—	—	—
—	—	—	—	—	—
×	×	×	×	×	×

Eventually a column will earn five advances and the first to do so is the winning "horse".

The banker notes the colour of the "horse" and pays out even money to all those who backed that colour. He appropriates all bets on the wrong colour or on losing columns, but he pays five times the bet on the winning column. Should there be a dead heat between two horses, the banker pays out two to one on each.

As may be imagined, the game can be particularly exciting towards the finish when two or three of the horses are going neck and neck.

The banker should be changed for each game.

34. PUT-AND-TAKE

Number of Players: Any number.
Cards: Full pack of 52 cards allowed for each nine players or proportion thereof.

IN addition to the cards, a supply of tokens and a large piece of card are needed. The card is divided into two portions—one is marked black and the other red. This card is then placed in the centre of the table, and the counters are divided out equally amongst the players.

A banker is selected, who shuffles the cards and deals out three cards to each of the other players. On completing the deal, the banker turns to the player on his left and says "Make your bet". The backer then puts one, two or three counters on red or black. That done, he turns his three cards face upwards. If there are two or three red cards and he backed red, the banker pays him as many counters as he laid, and the backer recovers his stake. But if there are two or three black cards, the banker takes the wager. Of course, if the punter has backed black, the opposite would apply.

The first bet being dealt with, the procedure is repeated in turn with each player round the table until every punter has made his bet.

Part one of the game being concluded, the backers now lay out their cards face upwards, and the banker turns the top card of the remainder of the pack.

If a punter has a card in hand of the same value (not suit) as the turned card he pays one counter into the pool; the next card is then turned and if a punter has a card of the same value he pays two counters into the pool; A player having the same value card as the third turn up pays three counters into the pool and so on until the tenth card is turned up and ten counters, where necessary, have been paid into the pool.

The procedure is now reversed. The banker will turn up the next ten cards one by one and will pay to any punter who may hold a card of similar value the number of counters dictated by the order of the turn up.

This concludes the game and the banker takes any counters which may be left in the pool. On the other hand should the pool "run dry" during the last part of the proceedings, he is obliged to pay out from his own funds.

The bank now passes to the player on the original banker's left, and thence in turn round to all the other players.

35. RANTER GO ROUND

Number of Players: Any number.
Cards: Full pack of 52 cards.

THIS is a good "ice-breaker" for a party. The dealer is selected by any of the approved methods and deals out one card to each player, including himself. The remainder pack he places on the table, face down.

The whole object of the game is for everybody to avoid being left with the lowest card in play (ace is low, and this game is sometimes called Chase the Ace). The game now proceeds as follows: —

(a) Each player looks at his card.

(b) The player on the dealer's left begins.

(c) If he is satisfied with his card he says "pass" and does nothing more.

(d) If he is not happy about his card he turns to player number two and says "change".

(e) Player No. 2 must change with him if asked, except when he holds a king, in which case he says "king" and does nothing more.

(f) If No. 2 says "king", No. 1 may then ask player No. 3 to change.

(g) If No. 3 should also hold a king, he says "king" and No. 1 must then continue to hold his original card.

(h) If No. 2 changes with No. 1 and likes the card he receives (i.e. if he knows it to be higher than the one which he exchanged) he will hold it and say "pass".

(i) If No. 2 is not happy with the exchange he turns to player No. 3 and says "change", which No. 3 must do unless he holds a king.

Play continues round the company until the last player on the dealer's right is reached. He may say "change" to the dealer exactly as already explained. If the dealer holds a king he does not exchange it, but cuts the remainder pack and gives the top card of the cut.

No matter what card the turn up is the dealer cannot come to grief unless it is a king. If it is a king, he pays a counter into the pool and no notice is taken of any of the other players' cards. If it is not a king, it becomes the card of the player on his right, whose original card is discarded.

If the dealer does not hold a king and wishes to change his card, either the one dealt or the card received from the player on his right, he cuts the pack and exchanges his card for the top card of the cut. If the turn-up is a king, the dealer forfeits one counter and the game is closed as already described.

Provided the dealer does not cut the pack and turn up a king, all the players' cards are now exposed. The player holding the one of lowest value pays a counter into the pool. If two players tie with lowest cards, they both pay. At the outset everybody should have three counters and, when they lose them, they drop out of the game. The player remaining in till the last takes the pool.

The deal passes after each round of play, and the cards should be well shuffled each time.

36. RUMMY

Number of Players: Up to eight or nine (more can play if additional packs of cards are allowed accordingly).

Cards: Two packs of 52 cards, with two jokers, making 106 cards in all.

NEARLY every family has their own version of rummy and it is very rare that you will find anyone else who plays the game of rummy with exactly the same rules as your own. The following method, therefore, is but one version and it is suggested that these rules are read and understood by every member before play is begun.

The two packs are shuffled well together and a dealer is selected by cutting (highest card cut takes the deal). The dealer deals out the cards singly to each player, until everyone has received seven cards.

The object of the game, which is the same in all versions, is to make runs or melds; that is to say, a consecutive run of cards, say six, seven and eight, of the same suit or a pair-royal (three aces, three kings, etc.).

After the deal is completed the remainder of the cards are placed face downwards in the centre of the table, or within reaching distance of all players, and the top card is turned face up and set beside the pack.

The player on the left of the dealer has the first play. He may take either the faced up card, or the card on the top of the pack which is, of course, an unknown quantity. Next he may, if he chooses, lay down any runs or melds which he may be able to make. It should be noted that whilst three cards in a run or meld is a minimum, a player may lay any number above that—thus if, say, he holds four or five cards of the same value, or a run of perhaps, three, four, five, six and seven, he may lay down the whole lot. A joker counts as any card, and in some versions the twos are also used as jokers, and this point should be decided upon before play.

The player having taken a card, laid down or not according to his hand, he must then discard one card, which is usually one which he does not want. But except in the last play, he must discard whether he wishes to or not.

In Rummy, a player may take either the top unknown card, on the left, or the top known card on the right. The card he throws out goes face up on the right

The play then passes to the next player on the left, and so on round the table, until one player is able to lay down all his cards which is "Rummy". When a player is "going-out", or "rummy-ing" he may either discard his last card or add it to a run or a meld, as he sees fit.

Once a player has laid down either a run or a meld on the table he may add any cards in his hands to other players' runs or melds. Thus, if for example, another player has a run of, say, eight, nine and ten of spades on the table, a player who has himself made a run or meld and who holds perhaps the jack of spades, may add this to the other player's run.

As soon as a player goes out, the hand is finished and the other players estimate the points value of the cards they still hold in their hands. Cards two to ten count points on their pip value (unless two is used as a joker, when it counts 15); court cards count ten points; aces count 11 points and jokers count 15.

Each player receives 300 points at the start of each rubber and at the end of each hand, the number of points according to the cards he still holds in his hand are *deducted* from his total number of points, and as a player reaches nil points he drops out of the game. The last person retaining any points is, therefore, the winner.

The deal rotates round with each hand and is always passed to the person on the left of the previous dealer.

To make the game more exciting, an agreed sum may be paid into the pool by each player at the beginning of the rubber, the winner taking the pool at the end; another variation is for each player to put in an agreed sum, as before, and as they drop out of the game having exhausted their 300 points, to buy themselves in for another hand at the same stake.

Note: Should any player be able to "rummy" on the first hand following the deal, the play continues round until each player has had a chance to complete one "go".

37. RUNNING WHIST

Number of Players: Up to ten.
Cards: Two packs of 52 cards.

THOUGH *Whist* is a game which has few equals, it has its drawbacks. One of which is that only four people can play at a time. Running Whist, while embracing the best features of the parent game, overcomes this draw-back, since any reasonable number may play together. Everyone plays for himself; there are no partners.

The cards are shuffled and dealt out singly to each player until about three quarters of the pack have been dealt. That is to say, if there are eight people playing, 11 cards each should be dealt; if there are nine, allow ten cards each; and if there are ten deal nine cards each, and so on.

The remainder of the pack of cards is set on the table face down and, when a player makes a trick, he takes the top card from the pack and places it with the rest of his hand. Thus when play has been in progress some little while, the various players hold hands of different sizes.

As soon as someone possesses no more cards he drops out of the game, and the others continue. At last the number is reduced to one and, because he has been able to remain the longest he is the winner.

Thus, it will be noticed that the making of tricks is only desirable because it helps to sustain a player's hand. Also it must be remembered that while playing, allow-ance should be made for the possibility of winning cards being dormant in the remainder pack. Lastly, since there are two cards of every kind, a rule has been made that when two exactly similar cards happen to be played to the same trick it is the first that beats the second.

38. SLIPPERY SAM

Number of Players: Any number.
Cards: Pack of 52 cards per every
                               ten players.

THIS game is very similar to Banker, but is considered
by many players to be the better game.

A banker is chosen by any agreed method, and he
allots a certain sum—it may be any amount he chooses,
but should not be so high as to embarrass any of the
other players—to constitute the bank. The cards are
then shuffled by the dealer and cut by the player on his
right; they are then dealt out three each to each player
and the remainder are set face downwards on the table
in front of the banker.

The first player now looks at his hand and it is his
duty to commence. He may do one of two things. He may
either "pass", in which case the next player on his left
takes the turn; or, he may bet any sum he likes (as long
as it does not exceed the amount in the bank) that
he has a card in his hand which will beat the turn-up.
It should be noted that, as yet, he has no notion as to
what the turn-up is. Directly the bet is made, however,
the banker turns up the top card and the player spreads
out his hand.

In deciding whether there is anything in the hand to
beat the turn-up each card is valued exactly as it is in
Whist, i.e. an ace ranks highest and a two lowest. In
addition the card to beat the turn-up must be not only
of a higher rank but of the same suit. There can be, of
course, no trumps.

When the first bet is concluded, the cards concerned
in it are thrown on one side and the turn-up goes too. It
is the turn then of the next player, who makes his bet
in an exactly similar manner and, when he has decided
on his course a fresh card is turned up. So the game

proceeds until every player has had an opportunity of making a bet.

There are very definite rules applied to the banker. The moment his bank is broken, he must withdraw and give the deal to someone else. If, however, his bank does well he cannot vacate his position until he has completed three deals. He *may* quit then; but he *must* go after four. During the course of the play the banker is required to keep the money on the table and not in his hand.

Any winnings must be added to the bank and nothing may be withdrawn except to pay out the bets. The usual procedure is for the bank to pass round the table, working to the left.

Slippery Sam is a game much beloved of card sharpers, and it is unwise to take a hand in a game which is being run by strangers—particularly on a train. Apart from that it is a game which provides very reasonable chances, since a punter sees his cards before he binds himself.

It must not be thought that the game is pure chance and nothing more. A quick head for figures and a facility for remembering the cards already played will go far towards making a good player. The law of averages plays a big part too.

When should a punter bet that he can beat the turn-up and when should he decline? These are questions which every player will be sure to ask. To answer this we set out a few figures. Suppose that a hand consists of three cards, all of which are tens. In the rest of the pack are the jack, queen, king and ace of the suits shown by the tens and a complete additional suit to beat the hand; i.e. twenty-five cards in all. Similarly, in the rest of the pack there are the nine, eight, seven, six, five, four, three and two of three suits which the hand will beat, i.e. twenty-four cards in all. Therefore, a hand of something better than three tens is needed to win according to the law of averages. Of course, allowances must be made for used up cards and it is here that skill and a good memory will tell.

39. SPECULATION

Number of Players: Any number.
Cards: Ordinary pack of 52 cards.

THIS is an old favourite which will continue to attract players probably as long as cards exist.

Before play commences, each player puts a counter into the pool. The dealer then gives three cards to each player, but none to himself. He turns the top card of the remainder pack and it belongs to him. The other players keep their cards face down and unexamined.

If the dealer turns up an ace, he takes the pool there and then, and that game is at an end.

If the dealer turns up a king, he may offer to sell it. There is only one ace of the same suit that can beat it and the ace may be asleep in the remainder pack. So the king is a good card and is worth almost as much as the contents of the pool.

Should the dealer not want to sell it, he calls "I challenge the board", and all players must turn their cards face up. If there is no ace of the same suit in any of the hands, the dealer takes the pool.

When the dealer's turn-up is any card other than an ace or king, the other players each turn only one card at a time. This is done in rotation round the table. The highest card of the dealer's turn-up suit takes the pool.

Any player turning a good card may offer it for sale to others who have not yet turned a card in the same round, and the play must be interrupted while the bids are proceeding.

The highest bidder for a card takes it and keeps it face up. He does not turn up a card of his own during that round.

Anyone turning the king of the dealer's turn-up suit may "challenge the board" and all hands have to be turned at once, whilst anyone turning the ace of that suit takes the pool and that game is finished.

A player looking at his cards at the wrong time falls out of the game and his cards do not count.

The deal passes at the close of each game.

40. SPOIL FIVE

Number of Players: Up to ten.
Cards: Full pack of 52 cards.

To the casual observer, Spoil Five appears to be needlessly intricate though, actually, the differences existing between it and *Whist,* which it closely resembles, make it a very pleasant variation of the better-known game. Indeed, Spoil Five is often regarded as the most scientific of all round card games.

Before sitting down to play Spoil Five there are one or two points that should be grasped. First, there is the curious ruling that the ace of hearts is always a trump and, as will be seen from the following lists, it is always the third best card to hold.

A second point to note is that the values of the cards change when a suit is trumps or when it is not trumps. Here are the values of all the suits. The highest card is given first; the lowest last:

Red Cards, when Trumps: Five, jack, ace of hearts, ace of suit if diamonds are trumps, king, queen, ten, nine, eight, seven, six four, three and two.

Black Cards when Trumps: Five, jack, ace of hearts, ace of suit, king, queen, two, three, four, six, seven, eight, nine and ten.

Red Cards, when not Trumps: King, queen, jack, ten, nine, eight, seven, six, five, four, three, two, also ace in the case of diamonds, but not of hearts.

Black Cards, when not Trumps: King, queen, jack, ace, two, three, four, five, six, seven, eight, nine and ten.

From all this it is apparent that the best card to hold is the five of whatever is trumps, the second best card is the jack of trumps, and the third best card is the ace of hearts.

When play begins, each player is dealt five cards— usually three together and then two together. Following that, the top card of the remainder pack is turned for trumps.

The next step is known as "robbing the trump". This is done in the manner here explained.

(a)   Should an ace be turned, the dealer throws out the card in his hand which he regards as of the least value and takes the ace. But, usually, he is only allowed to pick up the ace at the end of the first trick, though he announces his intention of doing so before the trick.

(b)   Should the turn-up not be an ace, the player holding the ace may make the exchange in the same way. Or, if he prefers not to make the exchange, he must ask the dealer to turn down the trump. If he fails to do this, his ace becomes the trump of lowest value, even when hearts are trumps.

When the "robbing" is completed the game proceeds, and each player tries to make tricks as in *Whist*. The rules about following suit are the same as in Whist, except that "revoking" (failing to follow suit) is permitted in certain circumstances. Here are the conditions on this point:

(a)   The five and jack of trumps and the ace of hearts need not follow suit to a lower trump that has been led.

(b)   The five of trumps may revoke to any trump that has been led.

(c)   No trump may revoke to the five of trumps.

(d)   The jack of trumps may revoke to any trump but the five of trumps.

(e) No trump, except the five of trumps may revoke to the jack of trumps.

(f) The ace of hearts may revoke to any trump but the five and jack of trumps.

(g) When hearts are trumps, the five and jack of hearts may revoke to the ace of hearts.

(h) When hearts are not trumps, and the ace of hearts is led, a heart need not follow it if one is held.

Should the first player to win three tricks elect to throw down his hand, he takes the pool; if he makes three tricks and plays on, making two or more tricks, he takes the pool together with one counter from each other player, If however, he does not throw down at three, but plays on and does not make five he gets nothing and the pool is left for the next round.

Each player puts one counter into the pool at the outset of every round; or some players prefer to supply the counters only when the pool is empty. The deal passes with each hand, in the usual manner.

41. SPOOF

Number of Players:	Any number.
Cards:	One pack for five or less players; two packs for more than five players.

To play Spoof, or Fan Tan as it is sometimes called, a plentiful supply of counters is needed.

There is no advantage in being the dealer, but the usual practice is for each player to take a card and the first to receive an ace becomes dealer for the first game. For subsequent games, the deal passes in rotation to the left to the original dealer.

F

All the cards are dealt out and, before examining his hand, each player pays one counter into the pool.

The object of the game is to be rid of one's hand as quickly as possible, and it is a rule that a player must play if he can do so. This rule eliminates the possibility of a player wrongfully withholding cards to the disadvantage of other players. Anyone who cannot play, when his turn comes, must "pass" and pay a counter into the pool. Only one card may be played at each turn.

The first card of any suit to be played must be a seven, and the opening of the game falls to the player on the dealer's left. If he can play a seven of any suit, he places it in the centre of the table. If he has no seven, he must pass—paying one counter into the pool. The next player on his left then has the opportunity of leading, and so on in rotation round the table until a seven is played.

When a player has laid down a seven, the next player may either play the six or eight of the same suit as the seven on the table, or the seven of another suit. Failing these alternatives he must pass. If he plays the six, he places it on the left of the seven; if he plays the eight, he places it to the right of the seven; if he plays the seven of a new suit, he puts it below and in a line with the seven already played.

Assuming that a player has led with the seven of diamonds and that the player following him has played the six of diamonds, the next in turn has the option of playing either the five or eight of diamonds, or the seven of another suit.

The foregoing examples should make the mode of play quite clear. From these you will perceive that on the left of each seven the cards from six to ace of the correct suit are played in descending order, while on the right of each seven the cards from eight to king are played in ascending sequence. The player who first gets rid of all his cards calls "Spoof", takes the pool and, unless otherwise agreed beforehand, receives payment of

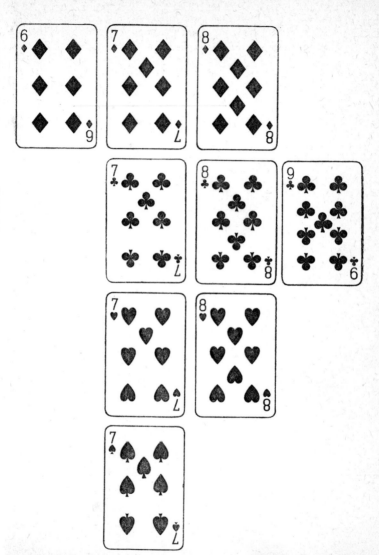

The lay-out for Spoof, showing how the game progresses

one counter for each card remaining in the hands of the other players.

In course of play it will be found advantageous to oneself to retain a seven as long as one can play another card. One must not, however, withhold a seven if it is the only card which can be played.

Penalties are provided for defaults. If after he has passed, it is found that a player could have played, he must pay three counters into the pool. If the card so withheld is a seven he must, in addition, pay five counters to the holders of the six and eight of the same suit.

42. STOCK EXCHANGE

Number of Players: Any number.

Cards: Allow one suit of cards per player, each suit consisting of the cards from ace to seven inclusive. Where more than one pack is used, the backs should be of the same pattern.

SHUFFLE all the cards well together, and then have them dealt to each player, one card at a time.

Each player should now look at his hand and consider what suit he will endeavour to complete.

With that decision in mind, the player on the dealer's left turns to the one on his own left and says "change four cards with me", or whatever number he needs to complete his chosen suit. Whatever number he may ask for, the other player must give him. The latter gives him the cards that are least useful for his own hand and hopes to receive, in exchange, some that will be more useful.

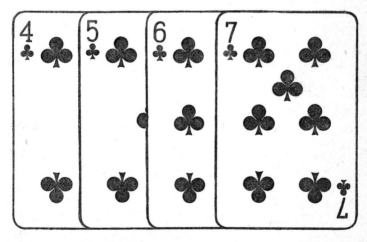

A complete Stock Exchange hand

The player who has surrendered the required number of cards, now turns to his left-hand neighbour and makes a similar request. So the game goes round until one of the players succeeds in holding a complete suit from seven down to ace.

On the first round a player may ask for two, three or four cards; on the second round he may ask for only two or three, and on the third round and any subsequent rounds he may ask for only two cards. Of course, in asking for two cards he must give two in exchange, and this often upsets his calculations, because he may already hold six cards towards the suit he has chosen. Consequently, the seventh card is usually the most difficult to get.

43. THIRTY-ONE

Number of Players: Any number.
Cards: Full pack of 52 cards.

THIRTY-ONE is a game of the same genus as *Vingt-et-un* but it contains additional elements and is an improvement on *Vingt-et-un* as a family game .

In Thirty-One, aces count eleven and court cards count ten; other cards count according to the number of their pips.

Before play is commenced each player pays an agreed number of counters into the pool. The dealer is selected, in the usual way, and the deal subsequently passes to each player in turn.

Three cards are dealt, one at a time, to each player and an additional hand of three cards to the centre of the table. This extra hand is exposed before play commences. The player on the left of the dealer, and the others in the customary rotation, may each exchange one card from their hands for one of those in the extra hand. The discard is put face upwards in the place of the card taken.

The object of the game is to make thirty-one, but the cards making it must all be of the same suit. Obviously the only cards possible are an ace and two court cards, or tens.

A typical "Thirty-one" combination

The nearest hand to thirty-one is a pair-royal (three of a kind) and a player may try for this instead. It counts thirty and a half, and should more than one player secure it the highest pair-royal is the best (i.e. three aces are better than three kings, and so on). After three of a kind, comes the highest total in any one suit.

The exchanging of cards goes on until some player is satisfied, which he signifies by knocking on the table, or by saying "content". It should be noted that a player *must* exchange or else knock. He cannot knock immediately after an exchange, but must wait until his turn comes again.

When a player has knocked, the others may each make one more exchange if they wish. The hands are then shown and the highest takes the pool.

44. VINGT-ET-UN (PONTOON)

Number of Players: Any number.
Cards: Full pack of 52 cards.

THIS game is probably the most well known and popular of all round card games.

To determine the banker, the cards are dealt round singly until an ace is turned; the player thus drawing the ace becomes the banker.

The main point of the game is to obtain two or, alternatively, more cards which total up to 21; or failing that, as near as possible to and under 21—on no account more than 21. Suits are immaterial and all the cards from two up to ten are reckoned at their face value. Each court card counts ten and an ace may be reckoned as one or 11 as desired. In the following description of the game the expression "ten" is used to indicate ten or a court card.

From the foregoing it will be recognised that the only combination of two cards which will give a total of twenty-one is a ten and an ace. This combination is termed a "natural" and, when held by a backer, entitles him to receive double the amount of his stake from the bank, unless the banker should also turn up a natural in the same round. It also gives him the right to hold the bank (which right he may sell, if he so chooses to the highest bidder), except if it is obtained on a split hand (described later); if it is turned up during a banker's first deal, or if the bank holds a natural at the same time.

The banker shuffles the cards and deals one face downwards to each of the other players in rotation, commencing with the player on his left, and lastly deals a card to himself. The backers examine their cards, replace them face down and bet according to their chances of securing 21 with a second card. Their stakes are placed on the table just in front of their cards.

When all stakes have been laid, the banker looks at his card and weighs up his own chance of securing 21 with a second card. If he considers his chance to be very good he may call "double", whereupon every backer is obliged to increase his stake to double the amount already laid. It may be mentioned here that it is not advisable for a banker to double the stakes unless his first card is an ace or a ten.

After this the banker deals a second card in the same way to each player, including himself. The backers again examine their cards, and any player who finds that he holds a natural lays his cards face up on the table. The banker also examines his hand and should he hold a ten and an ace he calls natural and lays his card on the table, whereupon any backer holding a natural must forfeit his stake, and double the amount of all other stakes on the table must be paid to the bank. All cards are then gathered up, shuffled and dealt again in the manner already described.

If the banker does not hold a natural, any player whose score is under 21 is entitled to receive further cards if he so desires. Backers who are satisfied with their score should place their cards face down on the table with their stake on top to signify that they do not wish to receive further cards—in other words that they are "sticking".

Any backer who hold two aces may split his hand; that is to say, he treats the aces as the first card of two separate hands, places his original stake against one, lays a fresh stake against the other, and calls on the banker to deal him two more cards. These cards are dealt face down, one against one ace and the other against the other ace. Thereafter, the backer treats each hand individually according to the ordinary rules of play.

It is important to note that, if a hand is to be split, it must be done at this stage of the game; it is not permissible once the banker has commenced to deal extra cards to ordinary hands. A banker may not split his hand.

The banker now attends to all backers needing further cards, dealing with the requirements of each in turn before passing on to the next player. Each of the backers is entitled to ask for one card at a time; he may either buy it by adding to his stake, in which case the card is dealt face down, or he may have a "twist", which is a card dealt face up without any further payment being made. He may not, however, buy a card after he has once had a twist, and when buying he may not add to his stake an amount greater than that originally laid. No more than three cards in addition to the two originally dealt may be obtained in this way, so that the maximum number of cards which any player may hold in one hand is five.

As each of the extra cards are dealt the backer reckons his increased score, and when this is twenty-one or what he considers a safe total on which to stand, he calls "stick" and places his cards face down on the table with his stake on top of them. In this connection it must be remembered that no one, not even the banker may "stick" at a score which is lower than 16, unless he holds five cards with a total which is under this figure.

If during the foregoing procedure, a backer's score exceeds 21, he calls "bust", throws in his hand (cards face down) and the whole of his stake which is on the table at that time is forfeited to the bank, while the banker places the cards at the bottom of the pack.

When all the backers needing extra cards have been dealt with in this manner, the banker turns up his own hand and takes extra cards for himself as required. If

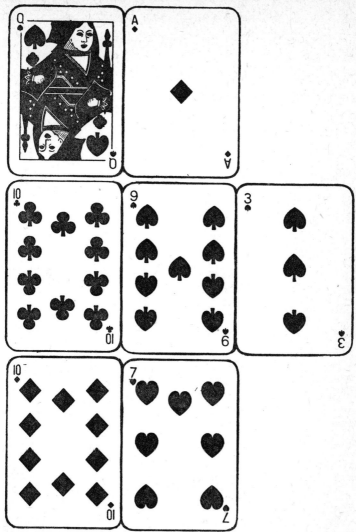

Three specimen hands at "Vingt-et-un". The player has
obtained a "natural" in the first hand. The second player has
gone beyond 21—he should not have asked for the third card.
In the third case, the chances are fairly good for "sticking"

his score comes over 21 he has to pay all backers still in the game the equivalent amount of their stakes then on the table, for all ordinary hands, but double the amount then on the table where a backer holds a natural or five cards with a score of 21 or less.

Should the banker make 21 with three or four cards, he receives all stakes with the exception of those in respect of a natural or five cards scoring 21 or less. For these exceptions he has to pay out as already directed. If his score is 21 or under with five cards, he pays out double for a natural and receives double all other stakes then on the table, excepting from a backer holding a similar hand, who merely forfeits his stake, as it then stands, to the bank.

The banker may, however, decide to stick at some score between 16 and 21. For example, at 19. In this case he announces that he will pay 20 and over. All backers whose score is less than 20 on a hand of not more than four cards forfeit their stakes then on the table to the bank, whilst the banker pays those whose score is 21 or less in five card hands, in the manner described for when his score exceeds 21.

Accounts having been settled, the backers' cards are gathered up and, unless a natural has been turned up, are placed underneath the banker's pack. The pack is shuffled only after a natural has been dealt.

Should more than one backer hold a natural in the same round when the bank does not hold a natural, the bank passes to the player who is first in turn from the left of the banker.

Before commencing the game it is advisable to place some limit on the amount which may be laid as the original stake—we suggest three counters as the maximum. Should it be desired to add more excitement to the game by playing for small stakes of money, counters can be bought from the host at the rate of a penny per dozen beforehand and converted again into cash at the end of a game.

When deciding, as a backer, the amount of one's stake, obviously it is worth going "all out" if one's first card is a ten or an ace—particulary *if* the latter. Generally speaking, one's stakes should decrease according to the lower face value of the first card; but in the event of this being very low, the possibiliity of obtaining five cards without exceeding a total score of 21 should not be overlooked.

45. WOOF-WOOF

Number of Players:	Any number.
Cards:	Allow a full pack to every five players, or portion thereof.

IF a real noisy game is wanted—one in which the youngsters may take a hand on an equal footing with their elders—this is the game.

The cards should be dealt out equally, one at a time, and if there is an odd amount left over these should be placed on one side and not used in that particular hand.

A leader is chosen, and he starts the game by announcing any card he likes. He names the rank but not the suit. Assuming he says "seven". The players glance at their hands, which should have been previously fanned out in order, and the first to find a seven and set it down on a pre-arranged spot on the table has rid himself of that card. Latecomers who own sevens must take their cards back and wait for another opportunity.

But as soon as "seven" has been laid and called, the chance of following with eight is open. And when eight has been put, it is the turn of nine, then comes ten, and so on up to the king; then without a break, it reverts to ace and the sequence is continued in this way until someone lays his last card and cries "woof-woof". The first to call "woof-woof" wins the pool which contains one counter from each player.

From this it will be seen that the object of the game is to dispose of the cards as quickly as possible. It is not necessary to place the cards on the heap, but it is important that they should be named and, in naming them a good deal of fun can be introduced into the game.

For instance, it may be ruled that whenever five is reached the layer must call out his Christian name, and when ten is laid the person laying it should say "one-thousand" or give the name of some European country; when perhaps the jack is laid, the name of a nursery rhyme character such as puss-in-boots can be given.

The penalty for a wrong call is usually a card taken from the remainder pack which, of course, delays the running-out of the defaulter. If there is no remainder pack, the defaulter is required to take back his card so that another player has the chance of playing a card of the same value.

Should a break in the sequence occur owing to the fact that there is a remainder pack, the leader must call another number at which a fresh run is to be commenced.